Stardust

SARA FRANCIS

No part of this publication may be reproduced in whole or in part, or stored in a retrieval system, or transmitted in any form or by any means, electronic, mechanical, photocopying, recording or otherwise, without written permission of the publisher.

ISBN:978-0-9989933-4-8

Copyright © 2018 Sara Francis. All rights reserved.

Cover image from Vincent Guth - www.unsplash.com

Artwork and Designs by Sara Francis

PUBLISHING

To my King.

Stardust

The stardust fell from the sky
gently kissing your skin.
It sparkled in your eyes
and your soul shone within.

It sprinkled down from heaven;
a gift of the angels.
To forgive us our transgressions
and help us love ourselves.

This blanket lay upon you
you gave it all your trust.
Your eyes and your heart too
enveloped in the stardust.

Your arms open wide.
Embrace it with great pride.

– Stardust

Sara Francis

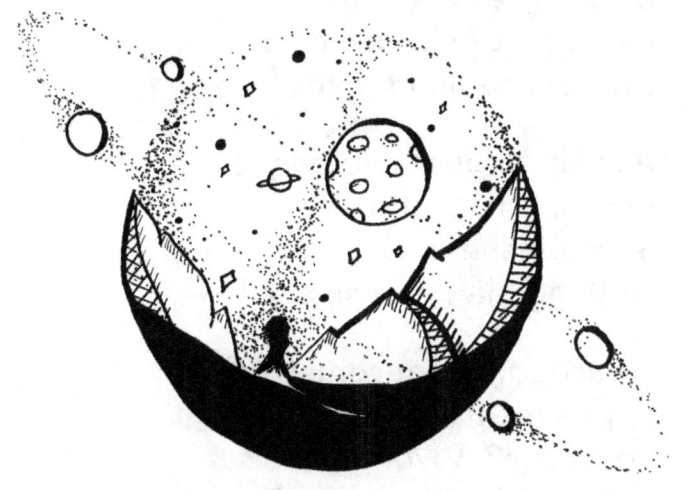

Stardust

Under the weight of words
my soul lies beneath.
No escape? No way out?
My past is haunting me.

As I flip through old pages
of scribbles and scrawl,
Senselessness? Brokenness?
Nothing made sense at all.

I reached out for something
to pull me from this.
Someone? Anyone?
Dying with my words it is.

— *Memories of Yesterday*

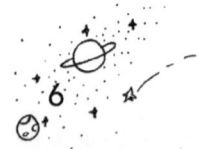

Sara Francis

Staggered all around.
Eyes locked on the ground.
Knees red, but not caring.
Don't dare to make a sound.

Inside, they're shouting.
Their cries, so abounding.
Not pain, but thanks
for what is surrounding.

— Adoration

Within me, my heart beats.
1...2...3...
How strange is this feeling?
My longing for thee.

— *Beginnings*

Sara Francis

"She says that these stories,
our life stories,
are of great value and should
never be forgotten.

Every day she reminds us that
one person and their story
is enough to change
the course of history.

"'Your story means something,'
she tells us,
'so write it!'"

— *Alison, Sami, and Aaron*
(The Isles by Sara Francis)

Nothing
compared to greats.

Nothing
compared to sick.

Nothing
compared to suffering.

Nothing
compared to You.

— What I Am

Sara Francis

The tears sparkle
in the light of candles.
Down her face they fall.
Their weight, too much to handle.

Trembling hands, weak legs.
Shallow breath in her chest.
She wonders why this happens
when she does her very best.

— Failed Attempts

Stardust

The keys beneath her thumbs.
The anger in her brain.
She knows what will be done.
She knows there will be pain.

Typing it all away,
her words a rainbow.
Slander, hatred, rage,
as if it's all she knows.

— Gossip

Sara Francis

The stars in the sky
look down on the earth with their
heads held up so high.

To them we are specks.
Small and insignificant
and there's nothing less.

Then they burn and fade.
Lifeless and cold they become.
With regret and pain.

— *The Prideful*

Stardust

The dangers that surround
never worried her.
Always smiling, happy eyes.
When the world was upside down.

— Mother Teresa

"A true princess
puts others before herself,
is obedient,
and virtuous
in all things."

— Abigail Quartermane
(The Mainland by Sara Francis)

Sara Francis

Knuckles turned white.
Nails dug in my skin.
Palms damp and wet,
My muscles tightening.

It slipped from my grasp.
Hot like burning fire.
My throat began to bleed.
I yelled and gripped tighter.

— Letting Go

Stardust

My soul wants to remain
here with you forever.
My love reaches for you,
the streams ending never.

But my love falls short
when I have to go away.
My responsibilities beckon,
but I only want to stay.

Are these callings from you?
Are they gifts for me?
The desires, the wonders,
these pains within me?

Grant answers to ease my mind.
For you, should I leave it all behind?

— Calling

Sara Francis

"Just as an artist looks
at a scene and paints,
so must the
writer.

Using a pen as his brush
and words as his colors."

— Sara Francis

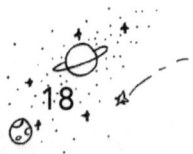

Sara Francis

The hum of engines
as they whip on by.
The stomping of feet.
The complaints, whines, and sighs.

The vibrations in my pocket.
The vulgarity on the boards.
Flipping through, all disordered.
Nothing moral, true, or pure.

— *Clamorous and Vile*

Stardust

Legs crossed beneath.
Hands folded so tightly.
Chin resting atop.
Eyes closed so gently.

Light lit her face,
but the fire's inside.
Silence is her strength.
In stillness, she's alive.

— *Gabby*

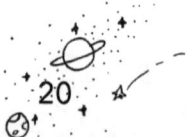

The fruit that is the hardest to peel
is usually the sweetest inside.

– People

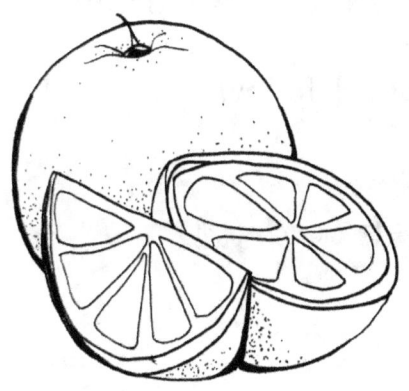

"Isn't the world amazing?
It's ruined and its people are
falling apart.

Yet, despite its brokenness,
we're still fighting to
make it better.

If there are still a few people
willing to find the truth,
the rest will follow."

— Mark
(The Isles by Sara Francis)

Sara Francis

A shadow cast upon him
like a storm with thunder and rain.
His mouth turned never upwards.
His eyes shone only pain.

— *Weights*

I take two steps,
it takes three.
I go one way,
it follows me.

My senses dim.
It grows larger.
I become weak
as it grows stronger.

— *Shadows*

"Don't worry so much about
the future
that you ruin the time
you have now."

– *Johanna*

(The Isles by Sara Francis)

Sara Francis

He comes secretly
within the night.
Face of radiance,
His clothes of pure white.

He opens his heart.
Offers to me.
It's wounded, destroyed.
Yet full of mercy.

— Faustina

Stardust

Teeth ever so sharp.
Scales hard as armor.
Red eyes shine in dark.
Its words like fire.

With broad sword in hand,
glist'ning in moonlight,
strike where it stands.
Send it to the night.

– Temptation

Sara Francis

The future holds something
which no one can see.
But we want to. We try to.
Impatient are we.

Worry, anguish
torment, no trust.

We rush it,
ruining it.
Thinking only of us.

— *Plans*

The crown upon Your head,
one moment shines so bright.
But suddenly, it changes.
Becomes a gory sight.

— *Gold to Thorns*

Sara Francis

You're not the one to gloat,
to say you're always right.
When we fall, you raise us.
When we succeed, you take delight.

— Father

Stardust

Fist thrown threw the wall,
screaming through my teeth.
Memories flooding back.
The ones that make me weep.

I know every moment
was meant for some purpose.
But it takes me too long
to find what the plan is.

— Regret

Sara Francis

Rugged, sharp, and fine was he.
Strength of a bear, stature of a tree.
Wispy locks with their own mind.
Eyes so cold yet glisten and shine.

Scorn, mockery, torment, oh!
Weights of which he must let go.
They upon his shoulders lie
To forfeit these would cost his pride.

– Tyrin

Stardust

As I sit in your presence,
gazing upon your face.
Your light emanating outward
illuminating the whole place.

Your words are so magnificent.
Your power so profound.
I sit in silence to hear you,
not daring to make a sound.

Oh, how is it you love me?
When you see what's in my heart.
To know you'd rather die
than with me ever part.

— *The Greatest Mystery*

Sara Francis

Stardust

Sara Francis

About

Sara Francis is a young woman with a passion for the written word. Along with inspiring people through poetry, she also is the author of a Sci-Fi trilogy, *The Terra Testimonies,* and the children's book series *The Adventures of Wobot.*

Through her writings and other works, Sara Francis is determined to light a torch in the darkness with the desire that people will do the same and make the world bright again.

To see more of Sara Francis' works, visit ***www.sara-francis.com***

www.ingramcontent.com/pod-product-compliance
Lightning Source LLC
Chambersburg PA
CBHW070443010526
44118CB00014B/2166